Discover India
State by State

OFF TO
WEST BENGAL

SONIA MEHTA

PUFFIN BOOKS
An imprint of Penguin Random House

PUFFIN BOOKS

USA | Canada | UK | Ireland | Australia
New Zealand | India | South Africa | China | Singapore

Puffin Books is part of the Penguin Random House group of companies whose addresses can be found at global.penguinrandomhouse.com

Published by Penguin Random House India Pvt. Ltd
4th Floor, Capital Tower 1, MG Road,
Gurugram 122 002, Haryana, India

First published in Puffin Books by Penguin Random House India 2017

Text, design and illustrations copyright © Quadrum Solutions Pvt. Ltd 2017
Series copyright © Penguin Random House India 2017

Picture Credits

P 6–7: Sundarbans low tide (Zvonimir Atletic/Shutterstock.com); P 10: Kolkata street (Radiokafka/Shutterstock.com); P 11: Woman selling jute products (Narayan Mitra/Shutterstock.com); P 22: Jorasanko Thakur Bari (glen photo/Shutterstock.com); P 26: Kirtan (© Calcutta Art Studio (British Library, cropped from original) [Public domain], via Wikimedia Commons); P 27: Chau dance (Rudra Narayan Mitra/Shutterstock.com); P 29: Durga idol maker (neelsky/Shutterstock.com), Saraswati idol (Dipak Shelare/Shutterstock.com); P 31: Taxis on Kolkata street (e2dan/Shutterstock.com); P 32: Mud village houses (ABIR ROY BARMAN/Shutterstock.com); P 36: Marble Palace (© Mjanich (File: Marble Palace Kolkata.jpg) [GFDL (http://www.gnu.org/copyleft/fdl.html) or CC-BY-SA-3.0 (http://creativecommons.org/licenses/by-sa/3.0/)], via Wikimedia Commons), Kalighat Temple (bodom/Shutterstock.com); P 41: Tree plantation worker (Pavel Svoboda Photography/Shutterstock.com), Fisherman (Rudra Narayan Mitra/Shutterstock.com); P 43: Jamdani sari weaving (KarimPhoto/Shutterstock.com); P 45: Decorated fish (© Arnab Sengupta)

The views and opinions expressed in this book are the author's own and the facts are as reported by her, which have been verified to the extent possible, and the publishers are not in any way liable for the same.

The information in this book is based on research from bonafide sites and published books and is true to the best of the author's knowledge at the time of going to print. The author is not responsible for any further changes or developments occurring post the publication of this book. This series is not a comprehensive representation of the states of India but is intended to give children a flavour of the lifestyles and cultures of different states. All illustrations are artistic representations only.

ISBN 9780143440765

Design and layout by Quadrum Solutions Pvt. Ltd
Printed at Repro India Limited

www.penguin.co.in

This is a legitimate digitally printed version of the book and therefore might not have certain extra finishing on the cover.

Hello Kids!

I'm so happy you are reading this book. India is an incredible country and there are lots of things about it that we never get to hear about.

I discovered India because my father was in the Indian army. He was posted to many places all over India—and we dutifully followed him. Can you imagine that by the time I was in the tenth standard, I had changed nine schools? Of course it was hard making new friends almost every year, but the good part was that I got to live in so many places. Right from Kerala, where I was born, to Kashmir, Jhansi, Shillong, Chandigarh, Goa . . . the list is long.

Every time I go to a new place, I feel amazed at how different each state is from the other—and yet, how similar. Did you know that we can see monuments from the Stone Age right here in India? Or that we have more than twenty official languages, and most Indians know three or four on an average? Or even that some of the world's most amazing scientific marvels were invented in India?

Oh, there are many, many, many fun and fantastic things about the states of India, which we simply must get to know.

So get your backpack ready, get set to meet some new friends, and join me on a fun trip as we **DISCOVER INDIA, STATE BY STATE**.

I hope you enjoy reading this book as much as I have enjoyed writing it. I would love to hear from you. So do write to me at sonia.mehta@quadrumltd.com.

Lots of love,
Sonia Aunty

Mishki and Pushka have come to visit Earth from their home planet, Zoomba. They have never seen such an amazing place. Zoomba doesn't have trees and mountains and rivers like Earth does. But the people look exactly the same. When they come to Earth, they meet a sweet old man whom they call Daadu Dolma. Daadu Dolma shows them all the wonderful places in India and tells Mishki and Pushka all about them.

Mishki and Pushka can't believe what they see. They have seen a lot of Earth, but they have never, ever seen a place like India.

They are off to explore India state by state :)

Mishki

Mishki is a curious little girl. She is always asking loads of questions. On her home planet, she is always getting into trouble for poking her nose into things that are not her business.

Pushka

Pushka is Mishki's brother.
He loves adventure. He is always ready
for a new challenge. Whether
it's climbing a mountain, or diving
into a cold, cold sea,
he is up for it.

Daadu Dolma

Daadu Dolma is a wise
old man who has lived on Earth longer
than the mountains and the seas. No one
knows quite how old he is, but
he certainly has been around.
He knows everything
about everything.

Mishki and Pushka can't wait. They have been so looking forward to this trip. They are eager to try the yummy sweets of West Bengal and see the famous Bengal tiger that they have heard so much about.

'Daadu Dolma!' says Mishki. 'Do we have to carry anything special to go to West Bengal?'

'Just keep your eyes and ears wide open because you are going to hear amazing music and see some wonderful sights,' says Daadu Dolma.

'And eat some delicious food!' adds Pushka.

'Yes, that too,' agrees Daadu. 'So keep your bags packed and let's go.'

Mishki and Pushka are set for their new adventure. They are

OFF TO WEST BENGAL!!!

Land ahoy!

Daadu, look. There seem to be so many different kinds of landforms here.

Yes, you are right. West Bengal is the only state in India that touches the Himalayas as well as the sea!

EAST, NOT WEST

Though this state is called West Bengal, it is actually in the eastern part of India. Why 'West' then? We'll find out a little later. But for now, let's meet West Bengal's neighbours.

West Bengal has a tropical climate.

FRIENDLY NEIGHBOURS

West Bengal has a curvy-wurvy shape. Odisha, Jharkhand, Bihar, Sikkim and Assam are all its Indian neighbours. It also has two foreign neighbours: the happy little country of Bhutan and a sister country called Bangladesh. Doesn't it look like West Bengal has its arm around Bangladesh? All of this sits right above the Bay of Bengal. What an interesting neighbourhood!

ON THE MAP

To see exactly where **West Bengal** is on the map of India, go to

http://www.mapsofindia.com/maps/india/india-political-map.htm

MANY DIFFERENT REGIONS

It's hard to believe that a single state can have so much variety. But that's how it is in this lovely area. They have the plains and the delta region, full of mangroves. The foothills of the Himalayas are also there, and they are dotted with charming hill stations from the British era. This area is called the Terai region.

RIVERS-A-PLENTY

The famous Hooghly River snakes its way through the state. Along the way, it shoots off tributaries with lovely names like Mayurakshi, Damodar, Kangsabati and Rupnarayan. There are rivers that flow down from the Himalayas too. The Teesta, Torsa and Jaldhaka are some of them. They bring cold, fresh water from the melting snow, making the soil rich.

FUN FACTS

State animal
Fishing cat

State flower
Shephali

State bird
White-throated kingfisher

State tree
Alstonia scholaris

MAGNIFICENT MANGROVES

There is a region in West Bengal called the Sunderbans. This area also loops into a part of Bangladesh. It is full of mangrove trees and shrubs that grow in the delta that has been created by the Ganga and other rivers. It is said to be one of the world's largest forests of its kind. Wow! Let's visit it right away.

Did you know?

Mangroves are small trees or shrubs that grow in regions with salty soil. Mangroves are terrific for wildlife.

A COMPLICATED NETWORK

The Sunderbans is crisscrossed with lots of muddy waterways, small mudflats and tiny islands. All these provide the perfect space for creatures great and small to live in.

A sad fact is that the Bengal tiger is endangered because of people hunting it. What a shame!

CREATURES OF THE DAY AND NIGHT

In this dark and rich forest, hundreds and hundreds of birds, animals and reptiles creep, flutter, run and sleep. There are more than 260 types of birds flapping around here, more than fifty-five kinds of reptiles crawling their way everywhere and nearly sixty types of mammals that make their homes in this deep, dark forest. Wow!

Fishermen at the Sunderbans

WILD AND WONDERFUL

There is amazing wildlife in the Sunderbans. There are rare crocodiles, turtles, water lizards and the famous Gangetic dolphins that swim around in its waters. This area is also home to some awesome slithery snakes like pythons, king cobras, banded kraits and Russell's vipers. And there are mammals like wild boar, spotted deer, porcupines and rhesus macaques that roam the Sunderbans.

HIDDEN CREATURES

Mishki is on an animal spotting spree. Help her spot all the creatures from the Sunderbans. There are eight creatures hidden in this grid.

Q	D	R	T	B	Y	S	Q	E	E	T	D	B	N	A
D	F	U	P	O	R	C	U	P	I	N	E	S	E	V
K	I	N	G	C	O	B	R	A	E	G	E	V	F	F
V	R	U	S	S	E	L	V	I	P	E	R	S	B	B
P	Y	T	H	O	N	S	E	T	Q	S	A	V	V	F
W	A	T	E	R	L	I	Z	A	R	D	S	W	E	R
W	H	C	S	Q	W	T	U	R	T	L	E	S	S	G
C	R	O	C	O	D	I	L	E	S	W	E	T	R	W

CITY CITY BANG BANG

West Bengal has lots of big cities. The biggest is the capital, Kolkata (or Calcutta, as it used to be called). But there are many other big and small cities. Darjeeling, Siliguri, Durgapur and Howrah are among them.

A busy Kolkata street

A 'toy train' takes people into Darjeeling.

TIME FOR TEA

As the hills slowly rise to meet the Himalayas, they create the perfect atmosphere for growing tea. West Bengal has huge, sprawling tea estates. Have you heard of Darjeeling tea? Aha! Here's where it comes from.

LOTS OF RICE

Thanks to all the rivers that are busy watering the plains of West Bengal, the soil is rich. It is perfect for growing rice. Therefore, rice is the largest crop that is cultivated here. In fact, most of India's rice comes from West Bengal.

JOYOUS JUTE

Lots of jute is grown here. A lot of our country's jute comes from West Bengal. Jute is like cotton, and people make things from it— like clothes, bags and mats.

TEA PUZZLE

Mishki is having a nice cup of Darjeeling tea. Help her match her teacup to the correct shadow.

Long, long ago

Well, it got its name only after India became independent. But, of course, like a lot of India, it has a long and rich history that is very, very ancient. Come, let me tell you all about it.

Daadu, is West Bengal a very old state?

Did you know? Bengal was originally called Vanga.

GREAT DYNASTIES

West Bengal used to be a part of the great Mauryan Empire, ruled by the famous kings Chandragupta Maurya and Ashoka the Great. The Mauryan Empire spread across almost all of India. The area that is now West Bengal was part of this empire.

Ashoka the Great

Chandragupta Maurya

A FIGHT FOR CONTROL

When the great Mauryan dynasty came to an end, other kings fought and controlled this region for a long time. These dynasties were called the Palas, the Pundras and the Senas. Of these, the Palas were the most successful.

Coins during the time of Vijayasena, a Sena king.

King Gopala of the Pala dynasty.

A CHIEFTAIN BECOMES A KING

The Pala dynasty ruled over Bengal (and parts of Bihar) for more than 400 years. This dynasty was founded by a man called Gopala, who was a local chieftain. Gopala, and his sons after him, did a great job of expanding the empire. Rampala was the last king, and the empire came to an end. The Pala dynasty supported Buddhism.

MUGHAL MASTERS

By this time, the Mughals had arrived in the north of India. Their reach began to spread east slowly, and soon, they captured the Bengal area. Under the Mughals, the region became a major centre for trade and industry.

Akbar II, one of the last Mughal emperors

FOREIGN FRENZY

Because West Bengal was close to the sea, and trade was flourishing, many foreign powers tried their hand at settling here. The Portuguese, the Dutch, the Armenians and even the French tried their hand. But eventually, it was the British who finally established themselves in this region.

A FIERCE BATTLE

The Mughal Empire had many nawabs (the title given to smaller kings) who ruled over smaller territories with the blessings of the Mughals. One such nawab was Siraj ud-Daulah. The British, under the leadership of a man called Robert Clive, defeated him in a fierce battle called the Battle of Plassey. They thus got complete control over Bengal.

Robert Clive after the battle

A NEW WAY TO RULE

The Mughal emperor at that time was Shah Alam II. He conceded defeat to the British and gave them the right to control the finances of Bengal, Bihar and Odisha. This was known as diwani and meant that the British collected and used the taxes that the people of Bengal had to pay.

Did you know?

Nawabs were Muslim royalty, who were known for their lavish lifestyles.

ODD, ISN'T IT?

There's one word or name that is out of place in each of the rows below. Circle it and help Mishki and Pushka solve the puzzle.

Portuguese	Dutch	British	Japanese

Bengal	Bihar	Odisha	Gujarat

Shah Alam II	Siraj ud-Daulah	Robert Clive	Donald Trump

FIRST BRITISH HEAD

An Englishman named Warren Hastings became the first head of British India. He was given the title of governor-general. The British decided to make Calcutta their capital. The region was called the Bengal Presidency.

Warren Hastings

THE FIRST SPLIT

The British felt that the Bengal Presidency was way too big for them to manage. So they decided to split it into two—West Bengal and East Bengal. It so happened that West Bengal mainly had Hindus, while East Bengal mostly had Muslims. The Indians didn't like the idea at all, but the British went ahead with the split anyway.

Now we know why it is called West Bengal even though it is in the eastern part of India!

WORD LADDER

Help Pushka climb the word ladder by changing the first letter as you go up.

T I G H T

Something that makes it bright

What you can see

Not left

Another word for 'perhaps', which also means strength

F I G H T

NEWS

We want to be free

All this time, the people of India were fighting to become free of the British rule. They wanted their own country back. The people of Bengal fought hard and played an important role in India's struggle for freedom.

Khudiram Bose (one of India's youngest nationalists), Aurobindo Ghosh, Bagha Jatin, Bipin Chandra Pal and, of course, Subhas Chandra Bose were some of the famous freedom fighters from Bengal.

FREE AT LAST

After a lot of small and large fights, the British finally agreed to give India its independence. The capital, by now, had been shifted from Calcutta to Delhi. Many, many Indians, led by Mahatma Gandhi, fought for India's independence. There was great joy and celebration when India finally became free.

People scrambling on to trains to get to safety

SADLY DIVIDED

After many discussions between the British and Indian leaders, it was decided that India would be divided into two separate countries—India and Pakistan. India would have more Hindus and Pakistan would have a mainly Muslim population. Thousands of people hurried across the border. It was a hard time for everyone. West Bengal became a part of India. East Bengal became a part of Pakistan (called East Pakistan). Many years later, East Pakistan became a new country called Bangladesh.

Anglo-Indians

THE BRITISH INFLUENCE

Because the British spent a lot of time in Bengal, there are still many streets and buildings in the state, especially in Kolkata, which have very British names. In fact, many British men married Indian women and this created a whole new community called Anglo-Indians.

AMAZING MAZE

Pushka and Mishki want to find their way out of this complicated maze so that they can take part in the freedom struggle too! Can you help them find their way?

Talk time

Talk time

I want to learn Bengali. I have heard it's a lovely language.
Yes, it's a very sweet language. Did you know that the language is also called Bangla? It is a primary language in many states in India like Odisha, Tripura, Jharkhand and Assam. It's also the official language of Bangladesh.

- Hello = Nomoshkar
- How are you? = Tumhi kemon achcho?
- I'm sorry = Aami khub dukhito
- Thank you = Dhonnobaad
- Nice = Bhalo
- What is your name? = Tomar naam ki?
- My name is Mishki = Aamar naam Mishki
- I don't know = Aami jani na
- Yes = Ha
- No = Na
- What? = Ki?
- How? = Kibhabe?
- That's okay = Theek achche
- What news? = Ki khobor?

Here's something interesting. In Bangla, the 'uh' sound is pronounced 'oh'. So the name Abhijeet will be pronounced Obhijeet.

LINGO SHINGO

Mishki and Pushka are practising the Bangla bhasha. Can you match the English words to the Bengali words and help them remember?

What? | That's okay | I don't know | What news? | How are you? | Nice! | What is your name?

Ki khobor? | Theek achche | Bhalo! | Tomar naam ki? | Ki? | Tumhi kemon achcho? | Aami jani na

A peep into their life

Daadu, when the language is so beautiful, there must be lots of amazing books to read.

Yes, indeed! Bengali literature is among the most interesting in the world.

WRITE AWAY

There were many famous Bengali writers who wrote wonderful books. Some of the earliest writers were Buddhist poet-philosophers. But from all of Bengal's brilliant authors, the one name that is the most famous is Rabindranath Tagore.

Jorasanko Thakur Bari, Rabindranath Tagore's childhood home

AWESOME

Rabindranath Tagore wrote hundreds of poems, songs, stories and plays. He wrote about ordinary peoples' lives and social issues. He even wrote stories for children. People read his books all over the world. In 1913, he won the Nobel Prize for Literature. His work has been translated into many languages.

Did you know?
Tagore has written the national anthems of both India and Bangladesh.

MANY GREAT WRITERS

Sarat Chandra

Bankim Chandra

West Bengal has produced many great writers. Bankim Chandra Chattopadhyay wrote many books. He also wrote India's national song, Vande Mataram. Another great writer was Sarat Chandra Chattopadhyay. He wrote several short stories about people in villages.

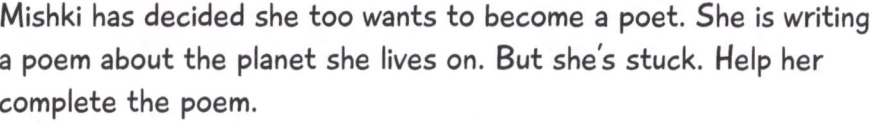

MISHKI THE POET

Mishki has decided she too wants to become a poet. She is writing a poem about the planet she lives on. But she's stuck. Help her complete the poem.

My planet is lovely, it is so green
It is the nicest place you've _____

The rivers are purple and the clouds are blue
You'd love my planet, come see it _____

The birds on my planet, they know how to swim
And the flowers do their exercise in the special Flower _____

Come to my planet, do come along
And together we can sing my lovely planet _____

23

MUSICAL BENGAL

When there is so much poetry and literature, can music be far behind? The people of Bengal love their music and have loved it for centuries.

LET'S GET CLASSICAL

Over hundreds of years, different people and dynasties lived in West Bengal. Each of them supported or created their own style. A Mughal emperor called Bahadur Shah loved music and was a big supporter of classical music. Under him, the Vishnupur style of music became well liked. It is still popular all over India.

Mughal emperor Bahadur Shah supported musicians.

PLAY BAUL

Baul is a mesmerizing style of folk music. It used to be sung by mystic minstrels—both Hindu and Muslim. These mystics would travel and sing their songs, which were all about how god is within us. The word baul means to be possessed by the wind. This was probably because the Bauls wandered like the wind. How interesting!

FOLKSY TUNES

There is other lovely folk music that is very popular in West Bengal. Kirtan, Bhatiali and Sari are some that enchant listeners with their simple tunes.

Dancing to Rabindra Sangeet

RABINDRA SANGEET

Rabindranath Tagore wrote lots of poems and songs. But did you know he was also a music composer? He wrote and composed many songs about nature, love, devotion to god and our nation. He did this in a particular style that was called Rabindra Sangeet. These songs have been translated into many languages. The people of Bengal love to sing and listen to these when they want to celebrate something, or when they are just relaxing. They even dance to these lovely tunes.

I will definitely try this!

Glass Jar Music

Pushka is so inspired that he is making his own musical instrument. You can make one too!

You will need

Six glass jars of different sizes, with metal lids

Water

A steel fork

Step 1 Fill the jars with different amounts of water and close them tightly.

Step 2 Tap the jars gently with the fork.

They will make different sounds. You can make up your own tune now!

TIME TO DANCE

A musical state like West Bengal would have many types of dance, of course! Especially folk. Let's see a few.

A DANCE OF THANKS AND PRAYER

This dance, also called the Kirtan dance, is a dance of prayer. People get totally engrossed as they move and sway to the religious songs that are played. These songs are called Kirtans.

Kirtan dance ←

A DANCE OF WAR

The Raibense dance is a vigorous one. Dancers hop and jump in circles, using shields, spears and trishuls (three-pronged spears) to express battle moves. Must be exciting to see!

TELLING STORIES THROUGH DANCE

Chau is one of India's most famous tribal dances, and many states have their own style. In West Bengal it is called Purulia Chau. The dancers wear masks and heavy costumes. They enact mythological stories through dance. There are loud drum beats, and the dancers move vigorously, leaping and jumping.

A DANCE OF EXPRESSION

The Lathi dance is one of expression. Celebration, love, anger, pain, sorrow, joy—all these emotions are expressed. It is usually performed during the Muslim festival Muharram. People perform this dance on streets and at country fairs. Young men hold long sticks that they twirl and spin to the beat of drums and cymbals.

In case you thought this state is only about music and dance, here's a snippet. People love football and have their own football clubs too.

One MASK Is DIFFERENT

Can you spot which of these Chau masks is different?

☐ ☐ ☐ ☐

CELEBRATION TIME

Like the rest of India, Bengalis too celebrate festivals with gusto. Diwali, Christmas, Eid—all these are celebrated, of course. But there are some festivals that are special to this region. Let's see a few of them.

PUJO

Durga Pujo is the biggest festival of all. For ten days, people pray to Goddess Durga. On the tenth day, amidst colourful processions, the idol of Goddess Durga is immersed in the river or sea.

THE STORY OF DURGA

There once was a buffalo demon called Mahishasura. He prayed to Lord Brahma, who gave him special powers. He became so powerful that he went around killing people and even gods. To stop him, the gods created a maiden to whom they each gave their most powerful weapon. This maiden was Durga. Durga rode a lion and killed Mahishasura.

Idol makers make mud or clay figurines of Durga weeks before Pujo. Many have been doing so for generations.

Did you know?
Durga Pujo is a celebration of the end of the evil Mahishasura.

PRAYING FOR KNOWLEDGE

Goddess Saraswati is the goddess of knowledge. Saraswati Puja takes place during the harvest season. People pray for a good harvest. This is the time of year when the yellow mustard flowers bloom. Yellow is also known to be Saraswati's favourite colour. So people wear yellow clothes, make sweets that are yellow and have feasts along with fervent prayer. This day is called Basant Panchami.

TOLLY HO

A majority of Bengal's movie industry is based in a place called Tollygunge. No wonder it's called Tollywood! But do you know something? Some of India's most famous and acclaimed movie-makers are from here.

A RAY OF BRILLIANCE

You must have heard the name Satyajit Ray. He was one of India's greatest film-makers. He was a writer, director, composer, designer— all rolled into one. He was a tall man—standing six feet four inches tall—and creativity was in his blood. Among his most famous films are *Goopy Gyne Bagha Byne* (a children's film) and *The Apu Trilogy*.

Satyajit Ray

Ritwik Ghatak

A DIFFERENT KIND OF CINEMA

West Bengal is also known for what is called parallel cinema. These are movies that are made not only for fun and entertainment but also have a message for people. People like Ritwik Ghatak and Mrinal Sen are just two in a long list of wonderful movie-makers.

Mrinal Sen

CROSSWORD TIME

Mishki now knows quite a lot about West Bengal. Help her crack the clues and solve the crossword to see exactly how much she knows?

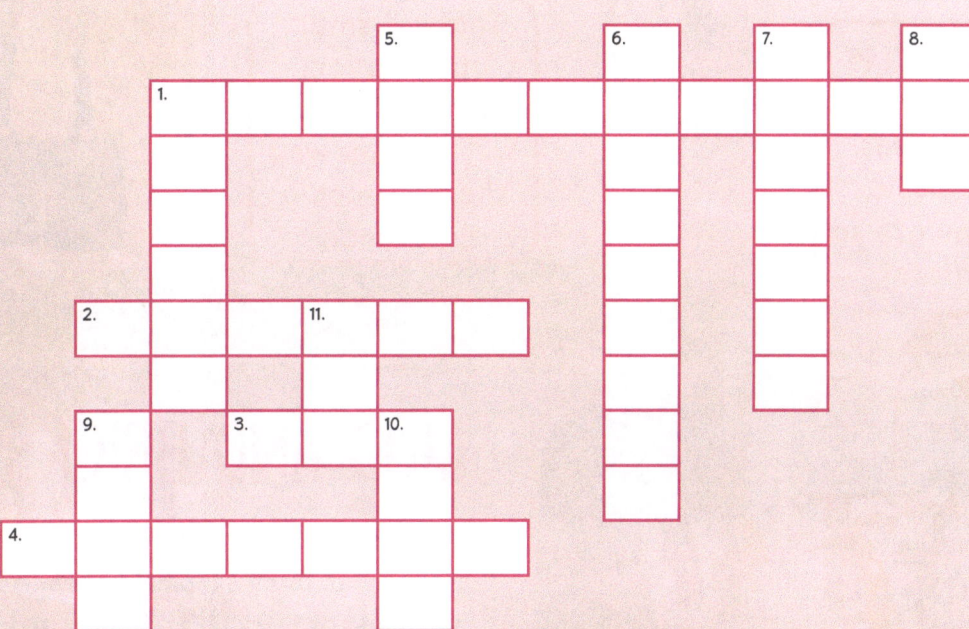

ACROSS

1. The name of the evil demon

2. _____ Panchami, when everyone cooks yellow food

3. The material that Durga idols are made of

4. Yellow _____ flowers bloom during harvest season

DOWN

1. _____ Sen made movies with a message.

5. She rides this beast as she kills the demon

6. The goddess of knowledge

7. The animal that the evil demon partly was

8. Satyajit _____—the brilliant movie director

9. The music sung by Hindu and Sufi minstrels

10. The goddess who killed the evil demon

11. Satyajit Ray's The _____ Trilogy

Bricks and Stones

Daadu, isn't it strange that some houses are so basic, and some are so elaborate?

That's a smart observation, Mishki. Come, I will tell you why there is such a difference.

MUD AND BRICKS

We've seen that a large part of West Bengal has farms. Typically, farmers' homes are made of brick, thatch, mud and bamboo. Large families live in a single room with small windows. And guess what? Pet animals like goats, lambs and even cows wander in and out of the house. Imagine that!

BUNGALOW BOOM

We know that the British made Calcutta their capital city. Many Bengalis began to adopt English customs. One of these was the style of houses they built. The word bungalow comes from the word 'bangla' which means 'belonging to Bengal'. The British built many bungalows that stand even today.

Chamkan Mosque

Temples at Kalna

TEMPLES, MOSQUES AND SHRINES

Jain Temple, Kolkata

Thanks to years and years and years of different kings, dynasties and religions, there are many temples, mosques and shrines that dot the state. Several of these are made of a material called terracotta.

Time to Sketch

Can you draw and colour this lovely colonial bungalow?

Draw and colour here

33

Standing strong

Daadu, such beautiful buildings! What are these?

Pushka, West Bengal has some amazing monuments, with lots of carvings and other details.

A MEMORIAL FOR A QUEEN

If you drive around the city of Kolkata, the local people will definitely point out one building with great pride. This building looks quite a bit like the famous Taj Mahal. But it is actually the Victoria Memorial. It was built in memory of Queen Victoria. It took fifteen years to build. It is a mix of British, Egyptian, Venetian, Mughal and Deccan architectural styles. Now it's a wonderful museum, with famous paintings and objects that Queen Victoria and other prominent people had in their homes and palaces.

SO OLD!

In Bishnupur, there is a temple called Rasmancha. It is believed to be one of India's oldest temples. During the Rash festival, people bring all their idols here and have a common prayer. Lovely, isn't it?

JUST LIKE ROSARY BEADS

You must have seen grannies pray with a string of beads. These are called rosary beads and usually have 108 beads. There is a group of 108 temples in Kalna that are just like these beads. A king, Maharaja Teja Chandra Bahadur, built these to pray to Lord Shiva. They are built in two circles: one within the other. How cool is that!

HIDDEN WORDS

How many smaller words can you make from the words given below? Jumble up the letters and see how many you can make. Mishki has done one.

QUEEN VICTORIA

TAR _____ _____ _____

_____ _____ _____

_____

A PALACE MADE OF MARBLE

The Marble Palace is a beautiful palace that was built by a rich Bengali merchant, Raja Rajendra Mullick Bahadur. He absolutely loved art. He used a mix of European, Chinese and traditional Indian building styles, with elaborate pillars, verandas and courtyards. In fact, his descendants still live in a part of the palace. And guess what? There is even a mini zoo in the gardens, which has peacocks, pelicans, hornbills, cranes and some monkeys and deer as well!

Lord Shiva's Tandav Dance

OOOH! SCARY STORY!

THE KALI TEMPLE

The amazing Kalighat Temple is dedicated to Goddess Kali. It has a fantastic story behind it. Sati was the wife of Lord Shiva. She married him against the wishes of her father, who was so upset that he insulted both Lord Shiva and his own daughter. Sati could not bear this and immolated herself—which means she burnt herself alive—on a pyre. Full of grief, Lord Shiva picked up the remains of his beloved wife and danced the dance of destruction. As he danced, a part of Sati's body, her foot, landed where the Kalighat Temple stands today! People from all over India come here to pray at this temple.

THE ARMENIAN CHURCH

Like so many Europeans, plenty of people from Armenia also came and settled in this part of India. As a matter of fact, they came much, much before the British did. They built a beautiful church as a place of worship. There are some famous paintings that show Jesus Christ and his followers.

LOST WORDS

Mishki has lost the words she learnt. Can you find all these in the grid below?

CHURCH   PALACE   KALIGHAT   SHIVA   SATI   PILLARS
PEACOCK   CHRIST   DEER   MONKEY   PELICANS   HORNBILL

P	I	L	L	A	R	S	D	H	V	A	C
E	W	S	B	C	S	N	B	G	B	C	A
A	X	M	O	N	K	E	Y	D	E	H	L
C	X	K	L	X	Z	W	U	W	S	U	E
O	O	K	A	L	I	G	H	A	T	R	G
C	P	U	K	B	X	Q	B	E	N	C	S
K	M	P	E	L	I	C	A	N	S	H	A
P	A	L	A	C	E	H	Q	D	V	N	T
X	S	D	A	S	X	R	X	V	B	N	M
B	H	O	R	N	B	I	L	L	P	H	B
V	I	N	M	K	A	S	W	D	E	E	R
Z	V	S	Z	S	A	T	I	D	C	C	V
W	A	E	G	J	K	L	X	L	W	R	B

CAST IN STONE

A TOWN, NOT A MONUMENT

You can't leave West Bengal without a visit to the world-famous Shantiniketan. Once upon a time, this area was called Bhubandanga because of a famous dacoit, Bhuban Dakat. Rabindranath Tagore's father, who was a wonderful man and a philosopher, opened an ashram on this land. He was an important leader of the Brahmo Samaj, a spiritual movement. People would come here to meditate and pray.

Did you know?

- Shantiniketan means 'the home of peace'.
- Satyajit Ray and Indira Gandhi (a former prime minister of India) were some of the famous people who studied here.

A SCHOOL WITH A DIFFERENCE

Over forty years later, Rabindranath Tagore began an open air school in Shantiniketan. As more and more students came here, it became an international university called Visva Bharati. Today, it is a place where Indian culture mixes with Western culture and everyone has one mission—world peace.

THE WONDER BRIDGE

The Howrah Bridge is probably one of West Bengal's most famous structures. It is an engineering marvel that the British built across the Hooghly River. It took seven years to build, which seems pretty quick. Why is this bridge special? There are no nuts and bolts in the bridge at all. It has been designed in a special way called riveting. It used thousands of tonnes of steel and is one of the busiest bridges in the world, with lakhs of people and cars crossing over it every day.

What a bridge!

Working hard

Daadu, what do Bengalis do for a living?

Well, many people in Bengal love art and literature. And, of course, food! But they also work very hard at what they do.

Food, food, food! We love it!!

HAPPY PEOPLE

People from Bengal are food lovers. Fish is a big part of their cuisine. Shopping for fish is as much fun as eating it.

FARMER, FARMER, WHAT DO YOU GROW?

Like a lot of India, farming is the biggest occupation. Farmers mostly grow rice—Bengalis love to eat rice. The other main crops are potato, sugar cane and oil seeds. Many farmers also grow jute.

LET'S GO FISHING

Bengalis love fish. It's no surprise that it is India's largest fish producing state. With all the rivers, mangrove areas and the sea, you can just imagine how much fish is caught here. There are lots of people who earn their livelihood by fishing.

TEA TIME

There are many large and wonderful tea estates—especially closer to the foothills of the Himalayas. That's because tea needs the cool climate of this region to grow. There are many people who work in the tea industry—as managers, tea tasters and tea pickers too!

FRUITY FLAVOURS

There are also some wonderful fruit orchards—especially towards the north of the state where apples, oranges and pineapples grow. This occupation is not as big as growing tea, but it's certainly a lovely one.

OFF TO THE MOVIES

Cinema is a big deal in West Bengal. Which is why the movie industry is huge too! Many people are employed in this business as actors, directors, writers and designers. Bengali films and film-makers are known all over the world for their brilliance. In fact, many Bengali actors and actresses have become famous in Hindi films too: Sharmila Tagore, Rakhee, Kishore Kumar and many, many more. How cool is that!

WEAVING MAGIC

Weaving has been an industry in West Bengal for hundreds of years and people have been doing this for generations. There are some amazing weaves called Jamdani, Baluchari and Tangail. Weavers weave magical designs that find their way on to saris and fabric. People all over the world adore them.

Jamdani saris are woven in West Bengal as well as Bangladesh

FISH SUDOKU

Pushka wants to go fishing. He needs help in placing the right fish in the empty squares. Each row, each column and each of the big four squares shown have one of each fish.

Yum yum yum

At last!!! I thought we would never come to this part. I'm so hungry.

You are always hungry.

Well, that's a good thing then. Because you are in for a feast.

FOOD: A SERIOUS BUSINESS

Bengalis take their food very seriously. Traditionally, a meal is divided into courses—just like in parts of Europe.

First: It starts with a bitter dish called shukto.

Second: Next comes shak—a vegetable preparation—and dal (pulses).

Third: Now comes the main part. It is usually a fish curry with rice, but mutton or chicken dishes are also served.

By the side: There are always accompaniments in the form of sweet and sour chutneys and aloo bhaja (grated and fried potato).

Sweet finale: And then the best part. Bengali mishti. No meal is complete without a famous mishti.

MACHER JHOL

This means fish curry and is a big part of Bengali cuisine. There are many kinds of freshwater fish that people love. The fish have interesting names like rui, koi, hilsa and bhetki.

Did you know?

Fish is so important in West Bengal that when a girl gets married, her family sends a decorated fish as a symbol of good wishes to the groom's family.

MUSTARD MANIA

A lot of the food is cooked using plenty of mustard. This might be an acquired taste, but if you like it, you are in for a treat.

Aha! Sweets! This needs a whole section. Let's start with the yummiest.

Yummmmy!!

RASGULLA

This amazing dish is popular all over India. These soft-as-cotton white balls of condensed milk are soaked in sugar syrup. When you bite into one, it explodes in your mouth. So delicious!

MISHTI DOI

This is a sweet yogurt that is made of milk and jaggery. You can eat it in lovely little earthen pots, which is how it is traditionally made.

SANDESH

This is a dish made of milk and sugar or jaggery. People shape it in different ways to make it even more interesting.

NOLEN GURER PAYESH

This is a yummy rice pudding made with rice, milk and jaggery. It is cooked and stirred and cooked and stirred till it becomes nice and thick.

SAVOURY FLAVOURY

Oh and, of course, there are some amazing spicy, salty snacks. Jhal Muri is a famous streetside snack made of spicy puffed rice. Puchkas are a cousin of the famous paani-puri (tiny fried puris filled with spicy water and lentils or spiced potatoes).

SWEET TREAT

Pushka loves everything sweet. Now that he's eaten all the Bengali sweets, he's on to other types. How many of each of the following sweet things can you find here?

Ice-cream cones	Cupcakes	Lollipops	Candy canes	Candies

What to wear?

I want to wear what they are wearing.

Yes, you can. But first you have to learn how to drape it properly.

DHOTI-SHOTI

Some men in West Bengal still wear a dhoti with a long kurta (a kind of long shirt). They throw a cloth over one shoulder too. Traditionally, men preferred crisp white dhotis and kurtas.

SOMETIMES A LUNGI TOO!

A lot of Bengali men prefer wearing lungis. This too is worn with a shirt or a kurta.

SARI WITH A DIFFERENCE

Many women wear saris, but in West Bengal the sari is draped differently from the rest of India. One edge of the sari is thrown over the shoulder. This loose end is called the pallu. Some women even tie their house keys to this! The most traditional of all is a white sari with a big red border. Women also sometimes wear a big red bindi.

A Bengali bride and groom

MODERN TIMES

Now, of course, men and women have started wearing modern clothes like shirts, trousers and jeans. But whenever there is a festival or a wedding, you will find everyone, men and women alike, dressed in their resplendent traditional outfits.

Same or Different

Look at this Bengali couple. Can you spot which two are the same?

A

B

C

D

Autograph, please?

It seems like West Bengal is full of learned and smart people.

That is absolutely true. Come, let's meet some of these amazing people.

SRI AUROBINDO

His original name was Aurobindo Ghosh. He was a spiritual leader, who believed in inner growth. He travelled the world and had so many followers. He built an ashram in a place called Puducherry, near Tamil Nadu.

SWAMI VIVEKANANDA

Swami Vivekananda was a great philosopher. He introduced the philosophy of Vedanta to the Western world. Did you know his real name was Narendranath Datta?

JAMINI ROY

Jamini Roy was an amazing painter. He had a unique style, and his paintings can be found in art galleries and homes all around the world.

Jamini Roy's painting

PANDIT RAVI SHANKAR

Pandit Ravi Shankar's full name was Rabindra Shankar Chowdhury. He was a world-renowned sitar player and composer. He came from a family of artistes. His brother Uday Shankar was a dancer. His daughter Anoushka Shankar is a famous sitar player.

RAJA RAM MOHAN ROY

Raja Ram Mohan Roy made a big difference in politics, social issues and education. He founded the Brahmo Samaj, through which he fought cruel age-old practices and made way for a fair society.

HRISHIKESH MUKHERJEE

This famous film director made some of India's best known Bengali and Hindi movies. He won lots of awards, and his movies were known for their humour that was mixed with a deep understanding of people.

KISHORE KUMAR

He was a talent powerhouse! An actor, singer, composer, director and writer, he was known for his crazy humour and genius. He acted in some of India's best-known comedies.

SUCHITRA SEN

She was considered to be one of the finest actresses to have emerged from India. She has acted in many world-famous Bengali and Hindi movies.

SAURAV GANGULY

Who doesn't know this cricket superstar? He was the captain of India for a long time and led the team to many victories. People affectionately call him Dada.

I want to be a cricketer like him.

Which One Is DIFFERENT?

We have met so many famous people from West Bengal.
From each row below, circle the one who is different from the rest.

| Saurav Ganguly | Suchitra Sen | Hrishikesh Mukherjee | Kishore Kumar |

| Swami Vivekananda | Sri Aurobindo | Raja Ram Mohan Roy |
| Pandit Ravi Shankar | | |

| Kishore Kumar | Suchitra Sen | Hrishikesh Mukherjee |
| Jamini Roy | | |

| Satyajit Ray | Mrinal Sen | Hrishikesh Mukherjee |
| Pandit Ravi Shankar | | |

Once upon a time . . .

Daadu, there were so many storytellers in this state. Tell us a fun story from Bengal.

Certainly. Here is a lovely old tale from Bengal.

THE TALE OF TETAN BURI AND BOKA BURI

Once upon a time, in a tiny village in West Bengal, there lived two sisters. Their names were Tetan Buri and Boka Buri. Tetan Buri was the clever sister. Boka Buri was the gullible sister.

Their parents had left them just three things—a cow to give them milk, a mango tree to give them fruit and a thick blanket to keep them warm.

Tetan Buri thought of a cunning plan. 'Boka Buri,' she said, 'we will share our belongings equally.

You take
the blanket
during the day, and I will
take it at night.' Boka Buri agreed
at once.

'I will take the lower half of the cow, and
you take the top half,' she continued.
Boka Buri agreed to that too!

'And as for the mango tree, I will take
the top half, and you take the bottom
half,' she said. Poor, innocent
Boka Buri agreed
once again.

As a result of this arrangement, unlucky Boka Buri got the blanket during the day, when it was hot. But she shivered at night while Tetan Buri slept warm and snug.

Boka Buri had to feed the cow, for she had the front of the cow. But Tetan Buri got all the milk.

And as for the mango tree, Boka Buri had to water it and change the mud. While Tetan Buri picked the juicy mangoes.

A wise old woman from the village saw what was happening. She called Boka Buri and told her what she needed to do.

The next night, when Tetan Buri took the blanket, it was soaking wet.

'Why have you wet it?' she yelled.

'Old Boudi from the village told me to wash it and give it to you,' explained Boka Buri. Tetan Buri had to shiver all night long.

The next morning, when she went to milk the cow, she got a big kick from the hind legs of the cow.

'Why is the cow kicking?' she yelled.

'Boudi told me not to feed the cow,' explained Boka Buri.

Suddenly, Tetan Buri saw Boka Buri taking a big axe.

'What are you doing?' she shrieked.

'Old Boudi told me to cut the tree in half. Then you can take the top half and I will keep the bottom half, just like you said.'

Tetan Buri realized that Old Boudi from the village had caught on to her trick.

'Stop, stop!' she protested. 'Don't cut the tree.'

Tetan Buri had learnt her lesson. And from that day on, she made sure she shared the blanket, the cow's milk and the mangoes equally with her sister.

TRAVEL DIARY

Have you enjoyed this trip to West Bengal with your friends Mishki and Pushka—and, of course, with Daadu Dolma?

Now you can make your own West Bengal diary. And if you ever visit West Bengal, make sure you take pictures and put them in the photo box.

The first place I would visit in West Bengal:

_____

If I ever meet Rabindranath Tagore, this is what I would say to him:

_____

The one dish I am definitely going to eat:

_____

The monument I think is the most interesting:

_____

The one famous person from West Bengal I would love to meet:

_____

If I were from West Bengal, my name would be:

_____

The festival from West Bengal that I think is the most fun:

_____

The five words that I think describe West Bengal the best are:

_____

_____

_____

_____

My West Bengal memories:

ANSWERS

page 9 Hidden Creatures

Q	D	R	T	B	Y	S	Q	E	E	T	D	B	N	A
D	F	U	P	O	R	C	U	P	I	N	E	S	E	V
K	I	N	G	C	O	B	R	A	E	G	E	V	F	F
V	R	U	S	S	E	L	V	I	P	E	R	S	B	B
P	Y	T	H	O	N	S	E	T	Q	S	A	V	V	F
W	A	T	E	R	L	I	Z	A	R	D	S	W	E	R
W	H	C	S	Q	W	T	U	R	T	L	E	S	S	G
C	R	O	C	O	D	I	L	E	S	W	E	T	R	W

page 11 Tea Puzzle

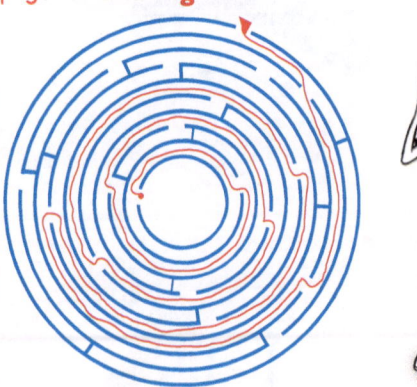

page 15 Odd, Isn't It?

Japanese, Gujarat, Donald Trump

page 16 Word Ladder

LIGHT   SIGHT   RIGHT   MIGHT

page 19 Amazing Maze

page 21 Lingo Shingo

What?—Ki?; That's okay—Theek achche; I don't know—Aami jani na; What news?—Ki khobor?; How are you?—Tumhi kemon achcho?; Nice!—Bhalo!; What is your name?—Tomar naam ki?

page 23 Mishki the Poet

seen, too, gym, song

page 27 One Mask Is Different

page 31 Crossword Time

ACROSS: 1. Mahishasura 2. Basant 3. Mud 4. Mustard

DOWN: 1. Mrinal   5. Lion   6. Saraswati
7. Buffalo 8. Ray   9. Baul 10. Durga
11. Apu

page 35 Hidden Words

Here are some of the words you can form: ace, act, air, ant, arc, are, art, ate, can, car, cat, virtue, victor, notice, retina, retain, recite, recent, nectar, neat, equate, entire, create, cornea, centre, carton, avenue, action, routine

page 37 Lost Words

P	I	L	L	A	R	S	D	H	V	A	C
E	W	S	B	C	S	N	B	G	B	C	A
A	X	M	O	N	K	E	Y	D	E	H	L
C	X	K	N	X	Z	W	U	W	S	U	E
O	O	K	A	L	I	G	H	A	T	R	G
C	P	U	K	B	X	Q	B	E	N	C	S
K	M	P	E	L	I	C	A	N	S	H	A
P	A	L	A	C	E	H	Q	D	V	N	T
X	S	D	A	S	X	R	X	V	B	N	M
B	H	O	R	N	B	I	L	L	P	H	B
V	I	N	M	K	A	S	W	D	E	E	R
Z	V	S	Z	S	A	T	I	D	C	C	V
W	A	E	G	J	K	L	X	L	W	R	B

page 43 Fish Sudoku

page 47 Sweet Treat

Ice-cream cones: 5; Cupcakes: 9; Lollipops: 9; Candy canes: 2; Candies: 15

page 49 Same or Different

B and D are alike.

page 53 Which One Is Different?

Saurav Ganguly, Pandit Ravi Shankar, Jamini Roy, Pandit Ravi Shankar